Celebrations!

Christmas

Anita Ganeri

Heinemann
LIBRARY

H www.heinemann.co.uk/library
Visit our website to find out more information about Heinemann Library books.

To order:
☎ Phone 44 (0) 1865 888066
▤ Send a fax to 44 (0) 1865 314091
▭ Visit the Heinemann Bookshop at www.heinemann.co.uk/library to browse our catalogue and order online.

First published in Great Britain by Heinemann Library,
Halley Court, Jordan Hill, Oxford OX2 8EJ
a division of Reed Educational and Professional Publishing Ltd.
Heinemann is a registered trademark of Reed Educational & Professional Publishing Ltd.

OXFORD MELBOURNE AUCKLAND
JOHANNESBURG BLANTYRE GABORONE
IBADAN PORTSMOUTH (NH) USA CHICAGO

Designed by Celia Floyd
Originated by Ambassador Litho Ltd
Printed by Wing King Tong in Hong Kong

ISBN 0 431 13790 0 (hardback)   ISBN 0 431 13798 6 (paperback)
06 05 04 03 02   06 05 04 03 02
10 9 8 7 6 5 4 3 2   10 9 8 7 6 5 4 3 2 1

British Library Cataloguing in Publication Data

Ganeri, Anita
  Christmas. – (Celebrations)
  1. Christmas – Juvenile literature
  I. Title
  394.2'663

Acknowledgements

The Publishers would like to thank the following for permission to reproduce photographs:
Andes Press Agency: Carlos Reyes-Manzo pp4, 15; Corbis: Kim Sayer p5, Archivo Iconografico p6, Phil Schermeister p14, Marc Garanger p20, Dave Bartruff p21; E & E Picture Library: J Allen p10, C Millington p12, Dorothy Burrows p19; Eye Ubiquitous: Skjold p9; Impact: Bruce Stephens p11, C E Mortensens p17; Sonia Halliday and Laura Lushington: p8; Trip: H Rogers pp7, 13, 16, 18

Cover photograph reproduced with permission of Christine Osborne Pictures

Our thanks to the Bradford Interfaith Education Centre for their comments in the preparation of this book.

Every effort has been made to contact copyright holders of any material reproduced in this book. Any omissions will be rectified in subsequent printings if notice is given to the Publisher.

Contents

Words printed in **bold letters like these** are explained in the glossary.

Happy Christmas!

Every year, on 25 December, **Christians** celebrate Christmas. This is when they remember **Jesus**' birthday. Jesus is very important for Christians. They believe that he is the Son of God. Jesus came to Earth to tell people of God's love for them and to save them from their **sins**.

Twinkling Christmas street lights.

Christmas is a very happy time. People decorate their houses with holly and mistletoe and hang tinsel and lights on Christmas trees. They send cards to their friends and give presents to each other. There are special Christmas services in church and delicious food to eat. People remember the Christmas message of peace on Earth and goodwill towards everyone. Many people who are not Christians join in the fun.

A frosty winter's day in Oxfordshire, England.

Christmas Day

Nobody knows exactly when Jesus was born. The first Christians chose 25 December as his birthday because it was the date of an ancient winter festival. On that day, people **worshipped** the sun to make it shine again in spring. The day was a holiday, with a great feast and games. People gave each other gifts, especially candles.

The Christmas story

Jesus was born about 2000 years ago in a country called **Judea**. An **angel** told Jesus' mother, Mary, that God had chosen her to have a special baby. She must call the baby Jesus. At that time, Judea was ruled by the Romans. They ordered everyone to go back to the town where they were born so that they could be counted.

The angel Gabriel appears to Mary.

Mary and her husband, Joseph, had to travel to **Bethlehem**. It was a long and tiring journey. When they arrived, the town was very crowded and there was nowhere for them to stay. Mary was worried. She knew that her baby would be born soon. Finally, a kind innkeeper took pity on them. He did not have a spare room but he did have a clean, warm stable. Later that night, in the stable, Jesus was born.

Bible story

The Christmas story is told in the **Bible**. This is the Christians' **holy** book. Luke's **Gospel** and Matthew's Gospel tell of Jesus' birth. John's Gospel talks about why Jesus' birth was so important.

Chidren looking at a **nativity** scene in a church.

It says that Jesus brought joy and light to the world. Luke, Matthew and John were followers of Jesus.

King Herod

On a nearby hillside, shepherds were watching over their sheep. Suddenly, the sky filled with light and an **angel** appeared before them. The shepherds were terrified. The angel told them to go to **Bethlehem** and **worship Jesus**.

Far away in the east, three wise men saw a bright star in the sky. The star was a sign that a new king had been born. The wise men followed the star to Bethlehem. They carried gifts for Jesus, of precious gold, **frankincense** and **myrrh**.

The three wise men brought gifts for Jesus.

King Herod was the king of Judea. He was furious when he heard about Jesus. He was afraid that Jesus would become king. He ordered all the baby boys in Bethlehem to be killed. But an angel warned Mary and Joseph of Herod's wicked plan. They took Jesus and escaped to Egypt. They lived there safely until Herod died a few years later.

Nativity plays

At Christmas, children often act out the Christmas story in church or at school. This is called a **nativity** play. They dress up as Mary, Joseph, shepherds, angels and the three wise men.

A boy acting the part of a shepherd in a nativity play.

Christmas is coming

Christians begin getting ready for Christmas about four weeks beforehand. This time is called Advent which means 'coming'. Christians start to look forward to celebrating **Jesus**' birthday and his coming to Earth.

The fourth Sunday before Christmas Day is called Advent Sunday. Many Christians go to church to take part in a special Advent service. They sing **carols** and listen to readings from the Bible about the coming of a **saviour**.

An Advent ring in a church.

In some churches, there is an Advent ring. This is a circle of **evergreens** with four candles, one for each Sunday of Advent. People light the first candle on Advent Sunday. A larger candle stands in the centre. It is lit on Christmas Day.

A girl opening her Advent calendar.

Advent calendar

Some children have an Advent calendar to mark off the days until Christmas. Try making your own Advent calendar. Draw a Christmas scene on a large piece of paper. Cut 24 windows in it. On another piece of paper, draw 24 small pictures to go behind each window. Then stick the two pieces of paper together. Starting on 1 December, open one window every day.

Christmas decorations

As Christmas gets closer, people start to put up their Christmas decorations at home and school. They might put up a Christmas tree or hang a green holly **wreath** on the door. Many of these Christmas customs are very old and have special meanings.

A holly wreath in a church.

People decorate their houses with **evergreens**. They remind people of God's everlasting love. They also remind people of spring, even in the frosty middle of winter. Some people hang up sprigs of mistletoe. This does not have a **Christian** meaning. But if you meet someone under the mistletoe, you are supposed to give them a kiss!

You will see Christmas trees everywhere, twinkling with lights. This custom started in Germany and came to Britain about 200 years ago. People decorate the trees with sparkling baubles and tinsel, and put a star or **angel** on top. The star reminds them of the star that shone on the night that **Jesus** was born. The angel is the Angel Gabriel who visited Mary.

The decorations come down on Twelfth Night (6 January). Then Christmas is officially over!

A beautifully decorated Christmas tree.

Thanking God

Christmas Day is a joyful time. Many **Christians** go to church to thank God for sending **Jesus** to them. They listen to **Bible** readings about Jesus' birth, praise God and remember the Christmas message of peace on Earth and goodwill towards everyone. Some people go to a special service on Christmas Eve. It is called Midnight Mass.

Midnight Mass in a church.

Music and songs are an important part of Christmas. People sing Christmas songs called **carols**. Below you can read the words of one of the best loved carols of all. Most churches and schools hold a carol concert. Carol singers go from home to home, singing carols in return for mince pies!

Children singing in a carol concert.

Away in a manger

Away in a manger, no crib for a bed.
The little Lord Jesus laid down his sweet head.
The stars in the bright sky looked down where he lay,
The little Lord Jesus asleep on the hay.

The cattle are lowing, the baby awakes,
But little Lord Jesus, no crying he makes:
I love thee, Lord Jesus; look down from the sky,
And stay by my side until morning is nigh.

Be near me, Lord Jesus; I ask thee to stay
Close by me for ever, and love me, I pray;
Bless all the dear children in thy tender care,
And fit us for heaven to live with thee there.

Cards and presents

At Christmas time, **Christians** send Christmas cards and give each other presents. Many people who are not Christians also like to exchange cards and presents. The presents remind Christians of the gifts that the wise men brought for **Jesus**. The gifts were gold, **frankincense** and **myrrh**. They were precious gifts that were fit for a king.

A girl opening her presents underneath the Christmas tree.

Do you believe in Father Christmas? Many people do. They think that he brings your Christmas presents on Christmas Eve. According to legend, the first Father Christmas, or Santa Claus, was St Nicholas, the patron saint of children. He was said to have been a very generous and kind-hearted man who helped people in need.

Father Christmas with a sack full of presents.

Christmas cards

Make your own Christmas cards. Decorate them with **angels**, stars and Christmas trees. Add some sparkly glitter or sequins to make them shine. Then write a Christmas verse inside.

Christmas dinner

A special meal, called Christmas dinner, is eaten on Christmas Day. Today, many people eat roast turkey, with roast potatoes, Brussels sprouts, cranberry sauce and stuffing. But people used to eat pork, goose or a big Christmas pie instead. You might have a Christmas cracker to pull while you are eating.

A family enjoying Christmas dinner.

For dessert, there is Christmas pudding. Traditionally, each member of the family took turns in stirring the pudding mixture. You had to make a secret wish as you stirred. Some people hide a lucky charm or a silver coin in the pudding.

Mince pies are little pastry pies filled with chopped-up fruit, raisins and spices. It is said that if you eat one for each of the twelve days of Christmas, it will bring you good luck in the coming year.

Another Christmas treat — a tasty Christmas cake.

Boxing Day

The day after Christmas is called Boxing Day. Long ago, people put money in boxes that were kept in the church. On Boxing Day, the boxes were opened and the money was shared out among the poor.

Around the world

Christians around the world remember **Jesus**' birthday at Christmas. But some people celebrate other special days around Christmas time. Some people give presents on 6 December which is St Nicholas' Day. Others have their main celebrations on Christmas Eve.

In Scandinavia, Christmas begins on 13 December. This is St Lucia's Day. Girls dress up in white with crowns of green leaves and candles on their heads. Everyone drinks coffee and eats sweet buns.

St Nicholas handing out gifts at a festival in Austria.

Some people celebrate on 6 January. This is called Twelfth Night or Epiphany. It is the day on which the three wise men visited Jesus. In Spain, people believe that the wise men pass by everyone's house to leave gifts. Children put out their shoes to collect them. The shoes are often filled with straw for the camels that carried the wise men to **Bethlehem**.

In Bethlehem, a silver star on the floor of a cave marks the place believed to be Jesus' birthplace. Over the cave stands the Church of the **Nativity**. At Christmas time, Christians come here from all over the world to remember Jesus' birthday.

Jesus' birthplace in Bethlehem.

Christian festival calendar

1 January	New Year's Day
6 January	Epiphany/Twelfth Night
7 January	Christmas Day in the Eastern Orthodox Church
14 January	New Year's Day in the Eastern Orthodox Church
2 February	Candlemas Day
February/March	Shrove Tuesday
February/March	Ash Wednesday/Lent
1 March	St David's Day
17 March	St Patrick's Day
March/April	Palm Sunday
March/April	Easter
23 April	St George's Day
May/June	Ascension Day
May/June	Pentecost/Whit Sunday
September	Harvest Festival
1 November	All Saints' Day
2 November	All Souls' Day
30 November	St Andrew's Day
November/December	Advent Sunday
24 December	Christmas Eve
25 December	Christmas Day
26 December	Boxing Day

Glossary

angel heavenly being who brings messages from God to people on Earth

Bethlehem town where Jesus was born

Bible the Christians' holy book. The part of the Bible called the New Testament tells the story of Jesus' life.

carols Christmas songs

Christian person who follows the teachings of Jesus

evergreens trees that do not lose their leaves in winter, such as holly and mistletoe

frankincense a sweet smelling perfume used in worshipping God

holy to do with God or a religious leader

Gospel There are four Gospels in the Bible, written by early Christians called Matthew, Mark, Luke and John. 'Gospel' means 'good news'.

Jesus Christ man who lived in Judea about 2000 years ago. Christians believe that he is the Son of God. They believe that he came to Earth as God in human form.

Judea land where Jesus lived; now Israel/Palestine

myrrh substance mixed with oil and used in religious ceremonies

nativity festival remembering the birth of Jesus

saviour someone who will save the world. Christians believe that Jesus is their saviour.

sins wrong-doings

worship to show love and respect for God

wreath decoration made of leaves, berries and flowers

Index

Titles in the *Celebrations* series include:

Hardback   0 431 13796 X

Hardback   0 431 13790 0

Hardback   0 431 13793 5

Hardback   0 431 13791 9

Hardback   0 431 13794 3

Hardback   0 431 13795 1

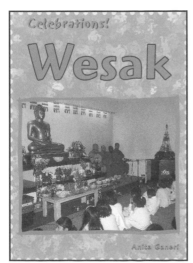

Hardback   0 431 13792 7

Find out about the other titles in this series on our website www.heinemann.co.uk/library